EUROPE'S TOP 20 STRIKERS

THEY ARE THE GLORY BOYS. These are the players who get paid loads of money to smash home goals on a regular basis to help earn their side trophies. Strikers come in all shapes and sizes, from giant, powerful hitmen who can terrorise defences with their sheer physical presence to small speed merchants who can nip behind a back line faster than you can shout "goal". Form is temporary but class is permanent – and the guys we have selected just ooze those special predatory skills which make them stand out from the crowd.

PUBLISHED BY

BOOKS LTD

PEDIGREE BOOKS LTD
BEECH HILL HOUSE
WALNUT GARDENS
ST. DAVIDS HILL
EXETER
DEVON EX4 4DH
books@pedigreegroup.co.uk

EDITOR: COLIN MITCHELL   **DESIGN & REPRO:** KEITH CHAMBERS   **WRITER:** JON REEVES

£6.99

EMMANUEL ADEBAYOR

EMMANUEL ADEBAYOR

FACTFILE

Full name: Emmanuel Sheyi Adebayor
Born: February 26, 1984, Lome, Togo
Height: 1.93m (6ft 3in)
Weight: 75kg (11st 8lb)
Clubs: Metz, AS Monaco, Arsenal

HONOURS

None

DID YOU KNOW?

● Emmanuel has often been referred to as "Baby Kanu" due to his resemblance to the Portsmouth and Nigeria striker.
● Adebayor scored after just 21 minutes of his Gunners' debut against Birmingham City at St. Andrews.
● He was sent off whilst playing in his first cup final for Arsenal. He received his marching orders against Chelsea in the 2007 Carling Cup after a mass player scuffle.

PROFILE

WITH HIS PACE AND POWER Emmanuel Adebayor is perfectly suited to the Premier League.

Since signing for Arsenal in 2006, the Togo forward has established himself as one of the most dangerous goal scorers in Europe. Bearing a striking similarity, in both appearance and playing style, to former Arsenal hitman Nwankwo Kanu, Emmanuel is strong in the air and skilful on the ball.

Adebayor began his career with Metz in France, but made his name with AS Monaco where he caught the eye of Arsene Wenger. The Arsenal coach saw plenty of raw potential that he could work with and parted with £3m to snap up the player.

Emmanuel was initially paired with Thierry Henry and his speed and strength proved a good match for the Frenchman's more silky style. When Henry left for Barcelona in the summer of 2007, Adebayor grabbed the limelight. He was a constant threat to defenders and finished top of the club's scoring charts.

His strength and close control allow him to hold off defenders and get shots away, plus his technical ability to score great goals provide Arsenal with a variation on their immaculate short passing game.

WHAT HE SAYS

"If you have to kick someone to win, that's not football, it's cheating. If you have to tackle hard that's okay, but tackle in a good way. Don't kick just because your opponent plays for Arsenal. We don't want a war on the football pitch."

SHOOT SAYS:

The Togo star scores goals with ease and is one of the most dangerous forwards in the Premier League. Emmanuel is the man!

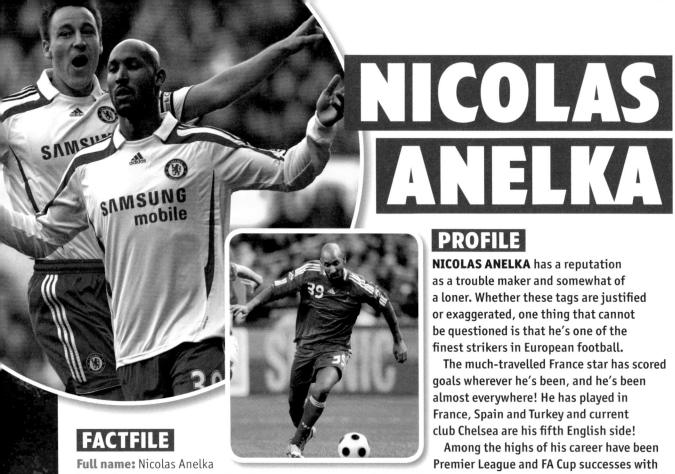

NICOLAS ANELKA

PROFILE

NICOLAS ANELKA has a reputation as a trouble maker and somewhat of a loner. Whether these tags are justified or exaggerated, one thing that cannot be questioned is that he's one of the finest strikers in European football.

The much-travelled France star has scored goals wherever he's been, and he's been almost everywhere! He has played in France, Spain and Turkey and current club Chelsea are his fifth English side!

Among the highs of his career have been Premier League and FA Cup successes with Arsenal, a Champions League crown with Real Madrid and European Championship glory with France. The lows have included frustrating spells at Manchester City and Bolton, where the goals flowed but so did middle table obscurity and relegation fights.

FACTFILE

Full name: Nicolas Anelka
Born: March 14, 1979, Versailles, France
Height: 1.87m (6ft 1in)
Weight: 77kg (12st 1lb)
Clubs: Paris Saint Germain, Arsenal, Real Madrid, Liverpool (on loan), Manchester City, Fenerbahce, Bolton Wanderers, Chelsea

HONOURS

European Championship: 2000
Confederations Cup: 2001
UEFA Champions League: 2000
Premier League: 1998
Turkish Premier League: 2005
FA Cup: 1998
PFA Young Player of the Year: 1999

DID YOU KNOW?

● Following several big money transfers, Anelka has become the most expensive footballer ever. After Chelsea signed him for £15m in 2008, his career moves totalled £85m!
● Nicolas is often referred to as "Le Sulk" due to his reputation for allegedly causing dressing room unrest at several clubs.
● Anelka currently wears the number 39 shirt for club and country.

WHAT HE SAYS

"I left for Madrid at 20 years old and I didn't really know how it would go. I didn't really know the club, but I don't regret it. It's good to have had in my life the times I had even though there were difficult times, there were some good times. It's good to experience different things."

SHOOT SAYS:

A real predator in the box, more than capable of scoring 20 goals a season, Anelka's move to Chelsea may have come just in the Nic of time for his career.

NICOLAS ANELKA

KARIM BENZEMA

KARIM BENZEMA

FACTFILE

Full name: Karim Benzema
Born: December 19, 1987,
Lyon, France
Height: 1.83m (6ft)
Weight: 73kg (11st 5lb)
Clubs: Olympique Lyonnais

HONOURS

Ligue One: 2005, 2006, 2007, 2008
Trophee des champions: 2006, 2007
Coupe de France: 2008
Lique One Player of the Year: 2008

He has pace and skill and knows where the goal is. His progression in recent years has been rapid and the Lyon striker is now one of the hottest properties in world football. Able to play on either flank or through the middle, Benzema is now the main man at the Stade Gerland.

The comparisons to Henry aren't unfounded as the youngster often drifts out to the left wing and dribbles inside. He is technically gifted, strong on the ball and can score from all angles and distances.

DID YOU KNOW?

● Karim qualifies to play for Algeria through his parents and could have played for the African nation before making his France debut.
● Benzema has a contract until 2013 with the French champions and, despite interest from Manchester United, has said he'd like to stay for at least one more season.
● When he made his international debut in 2007 he scored the only goal of the game as Les Bleus defeated Austria 1-0.

PROFILE

BILLED AS THE NEW THIERRY HENRY or the next Zinedine Zidane and already a target for Europe's top clubs, Karim Benzema clearly has a bright future.

WHAT HE SAYS

"It's a compliment to be compared to Zinedine Zidane but we are different players. There are players of my age who have lost it and started mucking up their careers. I have my feet firmly on the ground and know what I want to achieve."

SHOOT SAYS:

The next big thing in French football, kicking Karim has a bright future. Benzema will go far!

DIMITAR
BERBATOV

DIMITAR BERBATOV

FACTFILE

Full name: Dimitar Berbatov
Born: January 30, 1981,
Blagoevgrad, Bulgaria
Height: 1.89m (6ft 2in)
Weight: 79kg (12st 4lb)
Clubs: CSKA Sofia, Bayer
Leverkusen, Tottenham Hotspur

HONOURS

League Cup: 2008
Bulgarian Cup: 1999
**Bulgarian Footballer of the
Year:** 2002, 2004, 2005, 2007

DID YOU KNOW?

● When he joined Tottenham
in 2006 for £10.9m Dimitar
became the most expensive
Bulgarian player ever.
● Berbatov played in the
2002 Champions League
Final for former club Bayer
Leverkusen. The striker came
on as a second half substitute
as the Germans were defeated
2-1 by Real Madrid.
● Dimitar claims he learnt to speak English
by watching the three Godfather films!

PROFILE

THE BRILLIANT BULGARIAN has established himself
as one of the Premier League's most outstanding
performers since signing for Tottenham in 2006.

Berbatov is an elegant and skilful striker, equally
adept at creating chances as he is taking them. He
has an effortlessly precise first touch plus creative
and intelligent vision.

He is capable of playing his natural game amidst the
speed and intensity of the Premier League. He is also
strong in the air and often provides a direct option
if Tottenham are chasing
the game. As well as his all-round
game and technical class, the
Spurs star can boast an impressive scoring record.

One of coach Juande Ramos' biggest challenges
will be keeping his prized asset at White Hart
Lane and out of the clutches of a whole host of
top European clubs.

Rumours over a transfer to Manchester United
persist and a bigger stage like Old Trafford could
suit the Bulgaria captain perfectly.

WHAT HE SAYS

"When you first arrive in a new
country, you can take defenders by
surprise, but only for so long. They
know what to look out for now, and that is
another reason why I'm not sure you are always
seeing the best of me."

SHOOT SAYS:

The Godfather of White Hart Lane
could be a star wherever he plays.
But Tottenham fans certainly relish
their Berba King!

DIDIER DROGBA

FACTFILE

Full name: Didier Yves Drogba Tebily
Born: March 11, 1978, Abidjan, Ivory Coast
Height: 1.89m (6ft 2in)
Weight: 91kg (14st 3lb)
Clubs: Le Mans, Guingamp, Olympique Marseille, Chelsea

HONOURS

Premier League: 2005, 2006
FA Cup: 2007
League Cup: 2005, 2007
African Footballer of the Year: 2007
Ivorian Player of the Year: 2007

DID YOU KNOW?

- During his first two years at Le Mans "The Drog" was dogged by injuries with breaks to his fibula, ankle and two metatarsals!
- Didier's uncle, Michel Goba, was also a striker and played for French sides Brest, Dunkerque and Abbeville. He was also capped by the Ivory Coast.
- By scoring in the 2007 FA and League Cup finals, Drogba became only the third player to hit the target in two finals in the same season.

PROFILE

IN FULL FLOW Didier Drogba is one of the most dangerous strikers in the Premier League. Blessed with strength, skill and attacking instinct and the ability to use these attributes with great pace, he has been Chelsea's talismanic target man in recent seasons.

The Ivory Coast star took a season to settle in England but still played his part as Chelsea won their first league title for 50 years in 2005. The following season he became first choice striker as the Blues retained their Premiership crown.

His finest campaign was 2006-07 when Chelsea finished runners-up to Manchester United. Drogba almost kept Jose Mourinho's men in the title race single-handed, scoring plenty of crucial goals. Didier hasn't been entirely content in West London in recent times and a move to Italy or Spain always appears possible.

WHAT HE SAYS

"You need to have a football career to understand what we are feeling in a game. I tell you, people making judgments, sitting at home on the sofa, they are in another world."

SHOOT SAYS:

One of Africa's finest exports, Didier Drogba is one of the Premier League's most consistent performers. Beware of The Drog.

DIDIER DROGBA

SAMUEL ETO'O

SAMUEL ETO'O

FACTFILE

Full name: Samuel Eto'o Fils
Born: March 10, 1981,
Douala, Cameroon
Height: 1.80m (5ft 11in)
Weight: 75kg (11st 8lb)
Clubs: Real Madrid, Leganes (loan),
Real Mallorca, Barcelona

HONOURS

African Cup of Nations:
2000, 2002
UEFA Champions League: 2006
Spanish La Liga: 2005, 2006
Spanish Copa del Ray: 2003
African Player of the Year:
2003, 2004, 2005

DID YOU KNOW?

● **Samuel is the only player to have been named African Player of the Year in three consecutive seasons.**
● **Eto'o began his career at Real Madrid but struggled to make the breakthrough.**
● **He made his Cameroon debut at the age of just 15 against Costa Rica in 1996.**

PROFILE

ARGUABLY THE FINEST player to have come out of Africa, Samuel Eto'o is widely regarded as the best striker in the world. The Barcelona hitman is an expert finisher with a very direct style.

Eto'o boasts excellent pace and acceleration over a couple of metres. He is strong in the air, can hold the ball up well and works his socks off closing down opponents as Barca's first line of defence.

The Cameroon international took a few years to make his mark on European football following

a frustrating spell at Real Madrid. He was loaned to Leganes and Real Mallorca for first team experience. A permanent move to Mallorca soon followed, although Real maintained joint ownership.

His goals and consistent displays persuaded Barcelona to take a gamble on the Cameroon captain's talent and he joined them in 2004.

WHAT HE SAYS

"I have no idea where I will be in a few years' time, but at the moment I have a contract with Barcelona until 2010. There have been so many lies written about me. I would say 99.999 per cent of the things I have read about myself in the papers have been untrue."

SHOOT SAYS:

One of Barca's best, Eto'o is one of the most sought-after strikers in Europe. Sam the man knows where the goal is!

THIERRY HENRY

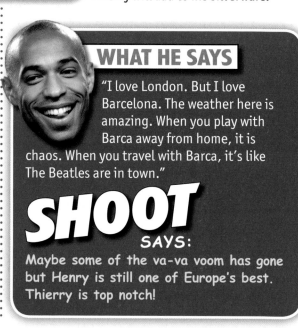

FACTFILE

Full name: Thierry Daniel Henry
Born: August 17, 1977,
Essonne, France
Height: 1.88m (6ft 2in)
Weight: 83kg (13st 1lb)
Clubs: Monaco, Juventus,
Arsenal, Barcelona

HONOURS

World Cup: 1998
European Championships: 2000
Confederations Cup: 2003
Premier League: 2002, 2004
French Ligue One: 1997
FA Cup: 2002, 2003, 2005

DID YOU KNOW?

● Thierry was runner up for the 2003 FIFA World
Player of the Year award. He lost out to fellow
Frenchman Zinedine Zidane. A year later he was
also voted into second behind Ronaldinho.
● He won the European Golden Boot in 2004
after scoring 30 league goals for Arsenal.
A year later he was the joint winner as he
and Diego Forlan each scored 25 times.
● Henry's first goal for Barcelona came
against Lyon in the Champions League
on September 19, 2007.

PROFILE

ONE OF THE FINEST players the
Premier League has ever seen, Thierry
Henry's performances during his eight
years with Arsenal were amazing.

The flamboyant Frenchman's
unique style dazzled defenders and
left supporters spellbound as he
scored spectacular goals and created
countless chances for team mates.

He left London as the Gunner's all-
time record goalscorer and signed for
Barcelona for £16m in summer 2007.
His first season in Spain produced 19
goals to make him the club's top scorer.

The lightning fast striker of days
gone by has now altered his game
slightly. Still a regular with France
and likely to form a frightening
partnership with Karim Benzema,
Thierry will add to his silverware.

WHAT HE SAYS

"I love London. But I love
Barcelona. The weather here is
amazing. When you play with
Barca away from home, it is
chaos. When you travel with Barca, it's like
The Beatles are in town."

SHOOT SAYS:

Maybe some of the va-va voom has gone
but Henry is still one of Europe's best.
Thierry is top notch!

THIERRY
HENRY

KLASS-JAN HUNTELAAR

KLASS-JAN HUNTELAAR

FACTFILE

Full name: Klass-Jan Huntelaar

Born: Drempt, Holland

Height: 1.86m (6ft 1in)

Weight: 74kg (11st 6lb)

Clubs: PSV Eindhoven, De Graafschap (loan), AGOVV Apeldoorn (loan), SC Heerenveen, Ajax

HONOURS

Dutch Cup: 2006, 2007

Huntelaar's predatory goalscoring instincts can be compared to Real Madrid striker Ruud van Nistelrooy. A tall forward, whose upper-body strength is developing all the time, Huntelaar is a tidy finisher, accurate with both feet and good in the air.

He lacks genuine pace, but is clever enough to find space using his excellent movement in the area. As well as the usual centre forward's goals, he is also capable of spectacular long range strikes or powerful volleys. He's one of the hottest prospects in Dutch football and has been linked to the Premiership.

DID YOU KNOW?

- The young hotshot is nicknamed "The Hunter" in his native Holland.
- Huntelaar began his career at Ajax's great rivals PSV Eindhoven but only made one first team appearance.
- Ajax paid Heerenveen £7.5m for the striker in 2005.

PROFILE

THE LATEST IN A LINE of hugely talented Dutch forwards produced at Ajax, Klass-Jan Huntelaar has the potential Holland stars such as Marco van Basten, Dennis Bergkamp and Patrick Kluivert have shown before him.

WHAT HE SAYS

"We shall see what happens about my future. For the time being I have only heard rumours. Everything will depend on any offers I receive and what is best for both me and Ajax."

SHOOT SAYS:

The Hunter is becoming the hunted as many of Europe's top clubs have him in their sights. Jan is pure Klass!

ZLATAN IBRAHIMOVIC

FACTFILE

Full name: Zlatan Ibrahimovic
Born: October 3, 1981,
Malmo, Sweden
Height: 1.92m (6ft 3in)
Weight: 84kg (13st 2lb)
Clubs: Malmo, Ajax, Juventus,
Inter Milan

HONOURS

Serie A: 2007
Dutch Eredivisie: 2002, 2004
Dutch Cup: 2002
Swedish Player of the Year: 2007

DID YOU KNOW?

● When he joined Ajax in 2001, Ibrahimovic
became only the fourth Swede to play for the
Amsterdam club.
● Zlatan is a Bosnian name which means "golden".
● Ibrahimovic became the most expensive
Swedish player of all-time when he joined
Inter from Juventus for £16.7m in 2006.

PROFILE

AT HIS BEST Zlatan Ibrahimovic is one of the most
gifted and dangerous forwards in European football
who can dominate defenders. At his worst he can be a
moody, inconsistent liability, as likely to give the ball
away as he is to score a screamer.
In recent years world football
has seen more of the super
Swede at his best as his game
has developed at Inter Milan.

Ibrahimovic can dribble the ball
and perform tricks as well as most
wingers and can also lead the line
like a traditional centre forward.

He first made an impact on the
European scene at Ajax where he
comfortably settled and was given
licence to roam up front. Juventus
snapped him up in 2004.

Ibrahimovic was a success at
the Stadio delle Alpi and won two
Serie A titles, which were later
taken away due to the financial
scandals that hit Italian football
in 2006.

Following Juve's relegation to Serie B, Zlatan joined
Inter Milan where his goals and creative style have
helped take the Nerazzurri to the next level.

WHAT HE SAYS

"With every year and every
championship I do better than the
last. This has been the best year of
my career."

SHOOT SAYS:

Lanky and extremely skilful, just think
Peter Crouch with girl's hair and a few
more tricks! Zlat can be a brat but is
also quality.

ZLATAN
IBRAHIMOVIC

FREDDIE KANOUTE

FREDDIE KANOUTE

FACTFILE

Full name:
Frédéric Kanoute
Born: September 2, 1977,
Lyon, France
Height: 1.92m (6ft 3in)
Weight: 69.2kg (10st 9lb)
Clubs: Lyon, West Ham
United, Tottenham Hotspur,
Sevilla

HONOURS

UEFA Cup: 2006, 2007
European Super Cup:
2007
Spanish Cup: 2007
**African Footballer
of the Year:** 2007

DID YOU KNOW?

● Freddie was eligible to
play for France and Mali
but elected to play for the
African nation in 2004.
● Kanoute was capped by
the French Under-21 team
whilst playing for Lyon.
● Freddie scored four goals in four games as
Mali reached the semi-finals of the 2004
African Cup of Nations.

PROFILE

SOME PLAYERS APPEAR made for certain clubs and
particular leagues, and it seems Freddie Kanoute and
La Liga side Sevilla are a match made in heaven.

After an inconsistent spell in England, playing for
both West Ham and Tottenham, Kanoute became
surplus to requirements at White Hart Lane and
joined the Spanish side in 2003.

The Mali star soon started hitting the net with
impressive regularity. Freddie scored all types of
goals and in all competitions, playing
a major role in the club's revival and
consecutive UEFA Cup wins in 2006
and 2007.

He has a good turn of pace, strength,
composure on the ball and a cool nerve
in front of goal. Able to score with his
head and either foot, Freddie is a constant threat
to defenders and is still improving.

Linked with a return to Spurs to reunite with his
former Sevilla boss, Juande Ramos, Kanoute may
fancy another crack at the Premiership.

WHAT HE SAYS

"It is an important time in my
career. At the moment I feel good
about things at Sevilla, but we'll
see. I would need to reflect a lot before taking
any decision."

SHOOT SAYS:

King Kanoute is a great all-round forward
who can score goals for fun. When he's
on form Freddie can be a nightmare for
defenders.

MICHAEL OWEN

FACTFILE

Full name:
Michael James Owen
Born: December 14, 1979, Chester, England
Height: 1.73m (5ft 8in)
Weight: 70kg (11st)
Clubs: Liverpool, Real Madrid, Newcastle United

HONOURS

UEFA Cup: 2001
European Super Cup: 2002
FA Cup: 2001
League Cup: 2001, 2003
European Footballer of the Year: 2001
World Soccer Player of the Year: 2001
PFA Young Player of the Year: 1998

DID YOU KNOW?

● Michael made his England debut against Chile in 1998 aged 18 years and 59 days. He became his country's youngest player of the 20th century.
● Michael is the only England player to score at four international tournaments. The Newcastle striker was on target at the 1998 and 2002 World Cups and the 2000 and 2004 European Championships.
● In 2001 Michael became the first Englishman since Kevin Keegan in 1979 to win the European Player of the Year award.

PROFILE

ENGLISH FOOTBALL'S MOST prolific goalscorer since Gary Lineker and one of the deadliest finishers in Premiership history! It's easy to forget how much Michael Owen has achieved in his career so far.

Recent injury struggles should not cloud his amazing record. Having made his Premier League debut as a 17-year-old at Liverpool and broken into the international scene a year later, Owen soon became the great goalscoring hope of English football.

Pace has been an important part of his game, but his composure in front of goal, movement, ability to be in the right place at the right time and strength in the air are also key attributes. The goals flowed again last season even from a slightly deeper role.

WHAT HE SAYS

"Everyone knows I'm a striker who scores goals and I'm best in the box, but I've enjoyed coming off the frontmen and I'm still getting into the box and scoring. I can play a bit more and when we're under the cosh it's always nice for the lads to have an outlet."

SHOOT SAYS:

Micky O has been rattling the goals in for years. He is a true Three Lions hero.

MICHAEL OWEN

ROBINHO

PROFILE

ONE OF THE MOST skilful players around, Brazil star Robinho has more tricks in his bag than a magician.

He can win games single-handedly when in the mood. Robinho has plenty of potential but has often flattered to deceive since signing for Real Madrid in 2005. Injury problems and fall-outs with managers and players have hampered his progress.

Elastic-legged, imaginative and able to perform step-overs and flicks at a great pace, Robinho has added end product to his game, linking up well with Ruud van Nistelrooy and Raul in an attacking trio at the Bernabeu.

He operates on either flank or as a deeper lying striker. A regular in the Brazil national team, the Madrid man often plays as a more orthodox striker and his pace and composure in front of goal has helped him achieve an impressive scoring record.

FACTFILE

Full name: Robson De Souza
Born: January 25, 1984, Sao Vicente, Brazil
Height: 1.72m (5ft 7in)
Weight: 60kg (9st 4lb)
Clubs: Santos, Real Madrid

HONOURS

Copa America: 2007
Brazil Campeonato: 2002, 2004
La Liga: 2007

DID YOU KNOW?

● Brazil legend Pele has labelled Robinho as his "successor".
● His nickname of Robinho actually means "Little Robin".
● Robinho claimed the 2007 Copa America Golden Boot after scoring six goals as Brazil won the trophy.

WHAT HE SAYS

"Everything is going for me right now. I'm creating chances and scoring goals. I'm very pleased with the football I'm playing but I'm always looking to improve. I hope to help the team as best I can, whether that is by scoring, by defending or by making the right pass."

SHOOT SAYS:

This South American starlet will certainly be one to watch in the next few seasons. Rampaging Robinho is red hot!

ROBINHO

CRISTIANO
RONALDO

CRISTIANO RONALDO

FACTFILE

Full name: Cristiano Ronaldo dos Santos Aveiro
Born: February 5, 1985, Madeira, Portugal
Height: 1.85m (6ft 11in)
Weight: 82kg (13st)
Clubs: Sporting Lisbon, Manchester United

HONOURS

Champions League: 2008
Premier League: 2007, 2008
FA Cup: 2004
League Cup: 2006
PFA Player of the Year: 2007, 2008
PFA Young Player of the Year: 2007
Football Writer's Player of the Year: 2007, 2008

DID YOU KNOW?

● Cristiano is one of only two players to have won both the PFA Players' Player of the Year and PFA Young Player of the Year awards in the same year, the other being Andy Gray in 1977.
● On March 19, 2008, Ronaldo eclipsed George Best's 40-year-old United record for the most goals scored by a midfielder in one season. Best scored 32 times in 1967-68.
● Cristiano was the first-ever Portuguese player at Manchester United.

PROFILE

CURRENTLY THE BEST PLAYER in the world, Cristiano Ronaldo has just had the season of his life. Scoring goals for fun, most of them spectacular, the Portugal ace has been in a league of his own.

Once labelled a one-trick pony with no end product, under the guidance of Sir Alex Ferguson Ronaldo has developed into a hugely skilled footballer.

He now scores and creates goals with ease. Cristiano has been given almost a free role in the United attack, with the hard-working Wayne Rooney and Carlos Tevez often tracking back when the team loses possession.

Although not an out-and-out striker, Cristiano's goalscoring record is the envy of most front men. King of the step-over and one of the most electrifying players in world football, Cristiano can tear defences apart and dominate games with his flair. He can pop up with a crucial goal, using either foot, his head or a spectacular free-kick.

WHAT HE SAYS

"I'm sure I'm playing better than I did one year ago. I have had more chances than ever, and that's because my team mates help me a lot. This is the best team I've played in since I arrived at Manchester United."

SHOOT SAYS:

There really is only one Ronaldo worth mentioning now as Cristiano is simply on another level. Rocket Ronny is no longer a winker, he's just a winner.

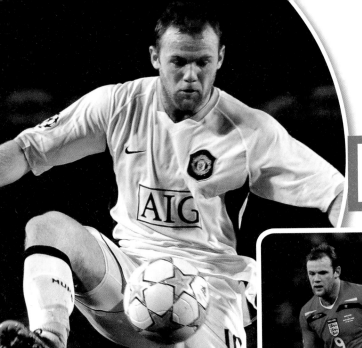

WAYNE ROONEY

success is often overlooked with Cristiano Ronaldo taking the credit. But United rarely lose with Wayne in the team. His work rate, competitive nature and hunger for success are vital ingredients to the squad.

The bustling forward combines strength, power and brute force with subtle finishing and measured passing. Can play as a central striker, in the hole behind a target man and on either side of a 4-3-3 formation.

Rooney works his socks off for the team, chasing back to help the midfield and defenders, and makes great runs and passes. Wazza is at his best during big games. Whilst Rooney isn't a prolific scorer, he creates chances for others.

As Fabio Capello attempts to rebuild the England team, Wayne Rooney will be central to his thoughts in making the Three Lions a real force.

FACTFILE

Full name: Wayne Mark Rooney
Born: October 24, 1985, Liverpool
Height: 1.78m (5ft 10in)
Weight: 78kg (12st 3lb)
Clubs: Everton, Manchester United

HONOURS

Champions League: 2008
Premier League: 2007, 2008
League Cup: 2006
English PFA Young Player of the Year: 2005, 2006

DID YOU KNOW?

● Rooney was England's youngest scorer. The Man United striker netted against Macedonia in 2003 when he was just 17 years and 317 days old.
● Wayne became England's youngest player when he made his debut against Australia in 2003 aged 17 years and 111 days. Theo Walcott broke this record in 2006.
● Man United fans call Wayne "El Blanco Pele", which translates as "The white Pele".

PROFILE

PROBABLY THE GREATEST talent England has produced since Paul Gascoigne, Wayne Rooney is one of the best all-round strikers in European football. The Roonster's contribution to Manchester United's

WHAT HE SAYS

"English football has improved so much in the past few seasons. We have proved we have the best league in the world, which is why we attract the best players in the world. I love playing here and I'm pretty sure that will never change."

SHOOT SAYS:

One of England's world-class performers, Wayne makes defenders wince when he's on top form. Rooney rocks!

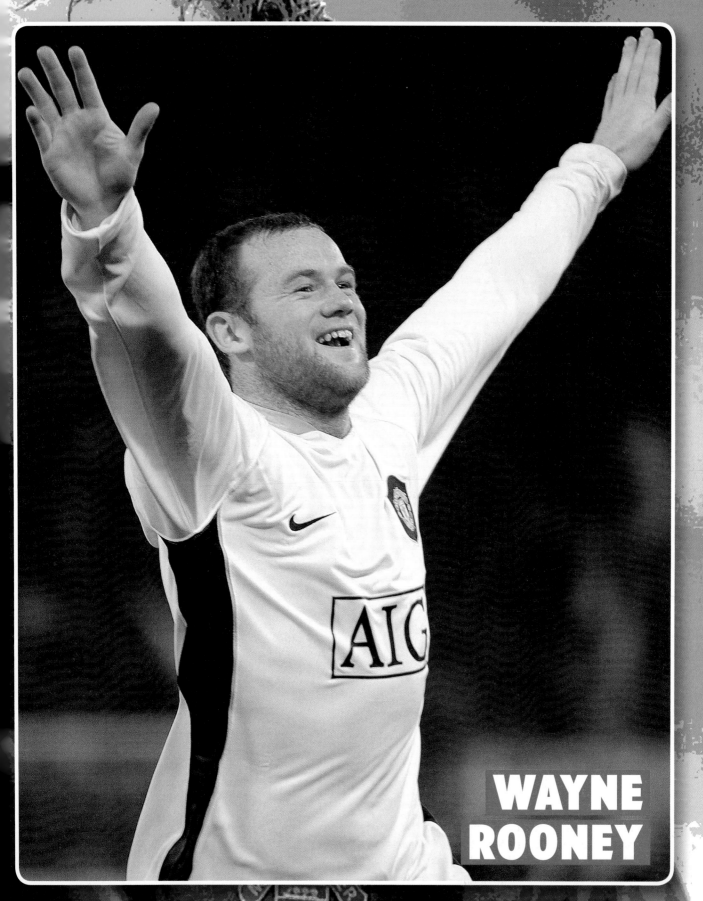

WAYNE ROONEY

CARLOS TEVEZ

CARLOS TEVEZ

FACTFILE

Full name: Carlos Alberto Martinez Tevez
Born: February 5, 1984, Buenos Aires, Argentina
Height: 1.68m (5ft 6in)
Weight: 75kg (11st 8lb)
Clubs: Boca Juniors, Corinthians, West Ham, Manchester United

HONOURS

Champions League: 2008
Premier League: 2008
Olympic Gold Medal: 2004
Intercontinental Cup: 2003
Copa Libertadores: 2003
South American Cup: 2004
Brazilian Campeonato: 2005

DID YOU KNOW?

- Carlos has a prominent scar from his right ear to his chest, after he was badly scalded with boiling water when he was a boy.
- Boca Juniors offered to have his scars partly removed but he refused saying they are part of him and he didn't want to miss any football!
- In 2003, 2004 and 2005, Tevez was awarded the South American Player of the Year by Uruguayan newspaper *El Pais*.

PROFILE

INVOLVED IN ONE OF THE biggest transfer scandals in Premiership history whilst at former club West Ham United, Carlos Tevez is now ensuring that he will be remembered for his goals and ability.

The stocky Argentine fired the Hammers to safety during 2006-07, despite question marks over his registration with the club.

Sir Alex Ferguson saw enough in the striker's on-field performances to convince him that Tevez was a United player and after a summer of negotiations

Fergie got his man on a lengthy loan agreement. Despite lacking pace and height, Tevez's tenacity and technical ability have helped him succeed in the Premiership.

Small in stature but with a huge heart and appetite for a battle, Carlos has linked up well with Wayne Rooney and Cristiano Ronaldo using his excellent passing and movement to create and take chances.

A goal-poacher in the area who also drifts deep and to either flank to get involved in play, Carlos is ideally suited to United's flexible attack.

WHAT HE SAYS

"The manager has not spoken in relation to signing a permanent deal. But obviously I would love to sign here. This is a great club and it would be fantastic for me to stay at United on a permanent contract."

SHOOT SAYS:

Carlos has been crucial to United's recent successes. When the big games come round expect the Argentine to step up to the mark. Tevez is top drawer!

FERNANDO TORRES

proved them wrong. Fernando's pace and strength were key factors, but his balance, dribbling speed and accurate finishing have been even more impressive.

A regular for Spain, Torres has shown maturity beyond his years by standing up to the more physical, experienced defenders and scoring vital goals for Liverpool. Strong in the air and tidy on the ground, Fernando links well with Steven Gerrard and could be the Reds first genuine 20-30 goals a season man since Robbie Fowler.

Torres' mere presence in attack keeps defenders occupied for 90 minutes, as they are well aware he can explode into action at any time. Give him an inch and Fernando will create a chance – as he proved with Spain's winner against Germany at Euro 2008!

FACTFILE

Full name: Fernando Jose Torres Sanz
Born: March 20, 1984, Madrid, Spain
Height: 1.85m (6ft 1in)
Weight: 69kg (10st 9lb)
Clubs: Atletico Madrid, Liverpool

HONOURS

European Championships: 2008

DID YOU KNOW?

● Fernando's nickname is "El Nino" – The Kid.
● Fernando was named Atletico Madrid captain at the age of 19.
● Torres made his full debut for Spain on September 6, 2003 in a friendly against Portugal. His first goal came against Italy on April 28, 2004.

PROFILE

THE SKILFUL SPANIARD
took the Premier League by storm in his first season in England. Many expected the young striker to take a while to settle following his £25m summer move from Atletico Madrid to Liverpool, but he

WHAT HE SAYS

"We haven't reached the standards expected of us. We've been inconsistent. When you consider the history of the club and the coach and the squad we have, we really need to improve if we are to fulfil expectations."

SHOOT SAYS:

Top Torres is one of the Premier League's most exciting strikers. After an awesome debut season a new Anfield hero is born. Can you hear the Kop Fernando?

FERNANDO TORRES

FRANCESCO TOTTI

FRANCESCO TOTTI

FACTFILE

Full name: Francesco Totti
Born: September 27, 1976,
Rome, Italy
Height: 1.80m (5ft 11in)
Weight: 80kg (12st 6lb)
Clubs: AS Roma

HONOURS

World Cup: 2006
Italian Serie A: 2001
Italian Cup: 2007
**Serie A Young Player of the
Year:** 1999
Italian Player of the Year:
2000, 2001, 2003, 2004

DID YOU KNOW?

● Totti won the European
Golden Boot for 2006-07
with 26 goals.
● Francesco is a UNICEF
goodwill ambassador,
and has released two
joke books to raise
money for the cause.
● He is Roma's record
goalscorer and the
most-capped player in
the club's history.

PROFILE

TRADITIONALLY AN ATTACKING midfielder playing
in the classic number ten role behind two strikers,
Francesco Totti has been transformed into a main
striker in recent seasons.

A true one club man, Totti has given incredible
service to his beloved Roma, staying loyal when the
team has struggled and other clubs have shown an
interest. A four-time Italian Player of the Year and
2006 World Cup winner with the Azzurri, Francesco

has been one of the few modern-
day skilful Italian playmakers to
fulfil his great potential.

With a sublime first touch and
great vision, Totti has been the
heartbeat of Roma since making
his debut as a teenager in 1993.
Famed for his long-range shooting and accuracy
from set-pieces, Francesco will probably be
remembered as Roma's best-ever player. He
has now retired from international football.

WHAT HE SAYS

"I am happy that I made this
commitment with Roma and I'll never
leave this club. I could have done it in the
past, but refused every time. And I'm proud of
myself. Roma is the best choice I could have
made in my career."

SHOOT SAYS:

Totti's Roman reign looks set to continue
as he reaches veteran status. All hail
Francesco!

DAVID TREZEGUET

PROFILE

ONE OF EUROPE'S most consistent and prolific strikers, Trezeguet is underrated by fans outside of Italy and France.

A tall, elegant forward whose composure in front of goal has helped club and country to glory, Trezeguet is deadly in the area. A graduate of France's famous Clarefontaine youth academy, he burst onto the scene playing alongside Thierry Henry at Monaco.

David's style is perfectly suited to the Italian game. A great goal poacher and header of the ball, Trezeguet has profited from playing with some excellent playmakers in Turin, including Zinedine Zidane, Alessandro Del Piero and Pavel Nedved.

Scored France's winner in the 2000 European Championships against Italy, netting a golden goal in extra-time.

But, having broke Italian hearts in 2000, his penalty miss in the 2006 World Cup Final gave them cause to celebrate.

FACTFILE

Full name: David Sergio Trezeguet
Born: October 15, 1977, Rouen, France
Height: 1.90m (6ft 3in)
Weight: 80kg (12st 6lb)
Clubs: Platense, AS Monaco, Juventus

HONOURS

World Cup: 1998
European Championship: 2000
French Ligue One: 1997, 2000
Italian Serie A: 2002, 2003

DID YOU KNOW?

- David is the highest-scoring foreign player in Juventus history.
- Trezeguet scored the 3,000th goal in Champions League history when he netted against Olympiakos in 2004.
- David grew up in Argentina after moving there from France at the age of two.

WHAT HE SAYS

"I am proud to link my name with Juventus for another four seasons. I made a decisive choice for my career and my life. This is a club which has given me so much and with whom I want to continue to win."

SHOOT SAYS:

David is a goal machine and one of the tidiest finishers in the business. "Trezegol" is a Serie A star!

DAVID TREZEGUET

RUUD VAN NISTELROOY

RUUD VAN NISTELROOY

FACTFILE

Full name: Rutgerus Johannes Martinus van Nistelrooy
Born: July 1, 1976, Oss, Holland
Height: 1.88m (6ft 2in)
Weight: 80kg (12st 6lb)
Clubs: FC Den Bosch, Heerenveen, PSV Eindhoven, Manchester United, Real Madrid

HONOURS

Dutch Eredivisie: 2000, 2001
Premier League: 2003
FA Cup: 2004
League Cup: 2006
La Liga: 2007, 2008
Dutch Player of the Year: 1999, 2000
English PFA Player of the Year: 2002

DID YOU KNOW?

- On January 23, 2007, van Nistelrooy announced his retirement from the Dutch team following a fall out with coach Marco van Basten. They later made up and van Nistelrooy returned to international football.
- During his time at Manchester United, Ruud scored six hat-tricks.
- Ruud is Manchester United's all-time leading goal scorer in Europe with 38 goals.

PROFILE

IT'S OFTEN SAID there is only one way to go after leaving Manchester United – and that's down! But former Red Devil Ruud van Nistelrooy appears to be the exception to this rule.

After leaving the English giants, Ruud joined Real Madrid in 2006. He has continued to score goals but has shown there is more to his game, playing a much varied role, coming deeper and getting more involved. At Old Trafford, van Nistelrooy's scoring record was phenomenal as he regularly scored 20-plus goals a season and broke Denis Law's European goalscoring record.

As United reclaimed their Premiership crown in 2007, the predatory striker played a crucial part in Madrid's La Liga triumph. Last season van Nistelrooy was again in impressive form, combining well with striker partner Raul and enjoying service from his fellow Dutchmen Arjen Robben and Wesley Sneijder.

WHAT HE SAYS

"Real Madrid has a fantastic set-up with marvellous people. The atmosphere at training is perfect– it's just wonderful."

SHOOT SAYS:

Van the man is one of the best strikers around. Include van Nistelrooy in the top 20? It'd be Ruud not to!

DAVID VILLA

FACTFILE

Full name: David Villa Sanchez
Born: December 3, 1981, Langreo, Spain
Height: 1.75m (5ft 9in)
Weight: 69kg (10st 9lb)
Clubs: Sporting Gijon, Real Zaragoza, Valencia

HONOURS

European Championships: 2008
Spanish Cup: 2004

DID YOU KNOW?

- David was Spain's top scorer during qualification for the finals of Euro 2008 with seven goals.
- Villa has been linked with a big money move to Chelsea, Arsenal or Liverpool.
- As a child David idolised former Barcelona and Spain midfielder Luis Enrique and often wears his number 21 shirt as a tribute.

PROFILE

SMALL IN STATURE but potentially one of Spain's biggest stars for the next few years, David Villa is one of the most exciting talents in La Liga. A fairly late developer, David only began to show his true class after moving to Real Zaragoza in 2003.

In a mid-table team he stood out as a natural goalscorer with lots of pace and excellent technique.

Spain's biggest clubs took an interest and Villa joined Valencia in 2005, the year he made his international debut.

Villa finished second-top scorer in La Liga in his first season, only losing out to Barcelona's Samuel Eto'o. The following season David formed a dangerous partnership with Fernando Morientes.

Last season the domestic goals dried up somewhat as Valencia struggled, but playing alongside Fernando Torres at Euro 2008 he looked very dangerous – and attracted a lot of admiring glances from England.

WHAT HE SAYS

"I have always listened when offers have been made. I have always made decisions about my career in conjunction with the club because I have a contract. I have to think about my future, and I will listen to everything."

SHOOT SAYS:

On form the sizzling Spanish hotshot can torment defenders and score for fun. Villa is a thriller!

DAVID VILLA

Six shooters who missed out...

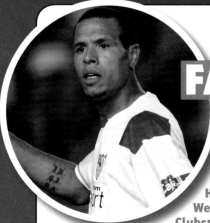

LUIS FABIANO

FACTFILE
Full name: Luis Fabiano Clemente
Born: November 8, 1980, Sao Paulo, Brazil
Height: 1.83m (6ft 1in)
Weight: 81kg (12st 7lb)
Clubs: Ponte Preta, Rennais, Sao Paulo, Porto, Sevilla

DID YOU KNOW?
● Fabiano was one of the scorers as Sevilla beat Middlesbrough 4-0 in the 2006 UEFA Cup Final.
● In 2005, Fabiano's mother was kidnapped by gunmen in Brazil. She was rescued by police 61 days later.
● Luis has been linked with moves to Chelsea, Arsenal, Manchester United and Liverpool.

WHY DID HE MISS THE LIST?
Although improving all the time, Fabiano has yet to show enough consistency to win a place in the Top 20. The Brazilian has played an important part in Sevilla's domestic and European success. Skilful, quick and great to watch, a move to a bigger club could see him make his mark.

ROBBIE KEANE

FACTFILE
Full name: Robert David Keane
Born: July 8 1980, Dublin, Republic of Ireland
Height: 1.75m (5ft 9in)
Weight: 73kg (11st 5lb)
Clubs: Wolves, Coventry City, Inter Milan, Leeds United, Tottenham Hotspur, Liverpool

DID YOU KNOW?
● During his career Robbie has been involved in transfers totalling £58m.
● Keano scored his 100th competitive goal for Tottenham in the 2-0 win against Sunderland on January 19, 2008.
● Robbie is the Republic of Ireland's record goalscorer after eclipsing Niall Quinn's record of 21 goals in 2004.

WHY DID HE MISS THE LIST?
Robbie is one of the most exciting strikers in the Premier League and when on form makes his team tick. Keano misses out because he probably doesn't score enough goals - although that may change now he is alongside Fernando Torres! He creates plenty of goals, is a team player and you can expect the Republic of Ireland striker to get even better.

RAUL

FACTFILE
Full name: Raul Gonzalez Blanco
Born: June 27, 1977, Madrid, Spain
Height: 1.80m (5ft 11in)
Weight: 68kg (10st 7lb)
Clubs: Real Madrid

DID YOU KNOW?
● On June 19, 2006, when he scored against Tunisia, Raul became the 18th player to notch in three different World Cups. He also scored in 1998 and 2002.
● Raul has worn the number seven shirt for Madrid since he was 19.
● He is the record goalscorer for the Spanish national team with 44 goals and counting!

WHY DID HE MISS THE LIST?
After one of his most impressive seasons in recent years, Raul only just misses out. His partnership with Ruud van Nistelrooy was crucial to Madrid's La Liga success and he continues to confound the critics who say he's passed his best.

They don't miss the target very often but these strikers just failed to make our current Top 20...

LUCA TONI

FACTFILE
Full name: Luca Toni Varchetta Delle Cave
Born: May 26, 1977, Pavullo nel Frignano, Italy
Height: 1.93m (6ft 4in)
Weight: 88kg (13st 9lb)
Clubs: Modena, Empoli, Fiorenzuola, Lodigiani, Treviso, Vicenza, Brescia, Palermo, Fiorentina, Bayern Munich

DID YOU KNOW?
● Luca captained Italy for the first time during a friendly against Ecuador on June 11, 2005.

● After scoring two goals Toni was named in the Team of the Tournament for the 2006 World Cup.
● Luca won the 2006 European Golden Boot after scoring 31 goals in Serie A.

WHY DID HE MISS THE LIST?
Despite an impressive couple of seasons at club and international level, late developer Luca misses out due to an inconsistent start to his Bayern Munich career. The Italy striker is still one of the most dangerous forwards around despite less than impressive performances at Euro 2008.

ROBIN VAN PERSIE

FACTFILE
Full name: Robin van Persie
Born: August 6, 1983, Rotterdam, Holland
Height: 1.82m (6ft)
Weight: 71kg (11st 2lb)
Clubs: Feyenoord, Arsenal

DID YOU KNOW?
● Robin's international debut was against Romania on June 4, 2005.
● He was Arsenal's top scorer in season 2006-07 with 13 goals.
● Van Persie was part of the Feyenoord side that won the 2002 UEFA Cup, beating Borussia Dortmund 3-2.

WHY DID HE MISS THE LIST?
One of the most promising young players in the Premier League, van Persie has yet to realise his great potential due to a series of injuries that have hampered his career. If he can stay fit the Dutchman could well be viewed as one of the very best players in the world in a few years – something Arsenal boss Arsene Wenger agrees is well within his sights.

YAKUBU

FACTFILE
Full name: Yakubu Aiyegbeni
Born: November 22, 1982, Benin City, Nigeria
Height: 1.82m (6ft)
Weight: 83kg (13st 1lb)
Clubs: Maccabi Haifa, Hapoel Kfar Saba (loan), Portsmouth, Middlesbrough, Everton

DID YOU KNOW?
● Yakubu is the highest-scoring African player in Premier League history.
● The Nigeria striker became Everton's record signing when he joined them from Middlesbrough for a club record £11.25m in 2007.
● Yakubu's Everton career got off to a great start when he scored on his debut against Bolton.

WHY DID HE MISS THE LIST?
The Yak is a regular scorer in the Premier League and on his day he can be a real handful for defenders. But he doesn't have enough of those days! Some fans question his work rate and desire but he is more of a team player under David Moyes.